The Way, the Truth, and the Life

Daily Devotions, Volume 6

Dr Andrew C S Koh

Published by Dr. Andrew C S Koh, 2023.

Copyright

All scripture quotations are from the World English Bible unless stated otherwise.

Scan QR code below to get a free e-book.

Table of Contents

To my beloved wife, Wai Yin, whose love and unwavering support have been the foundation of everything I do.

To my sons, who have brought joy and purpose into my life.

To my daughters-in-law, who have enriched our family with their warmth and kindness.

To my grandsons and granddaughters, the light of my life, who remind me daily of the beauty and wonder of the world.

And above all, to the glory of God, whose grace has guided me through every step of my journey.

This book is for you all.

Matthew 4:4- *Man shall not live by bread alone, but by every word that comes from the mouth of God.*

Preface

Welcome to 'The Way, the Truth, and the Life' devotional book! Join me on a journey of faith, hope, and spiritual growth. I hope this book will inspire and guide you in your relationship with God. Remember, Jesus is always with us, supporting us, and giving us strength, as we face the ups and downs of life. Remember the power of prayer, God's steadfast love, and the transformative nature of a faith-centered life. May it be a blessing to you, and may you be inspired to walk this journey of faith with unwavering determination and trust in the Lord. This book will help you connect with God and live a fulfilling life following His teachings. Let us embark on this spiritual journey with open hearts and minds, ready to receive the deep wisdom and divine grace that flow abundantly through the teachings of Jesus Christ. Let us seek His guidance, meditate on His words, and allow His truth to illuminate our lives, transforming us from within. May this inspirational book awaken a deepened sense of purpose within you, igniting an unwavering faith that sustains your pursuit of righteousness and a profound love that embraces and uplifts others. Find solace, inspiration, and spiritual sustenance while contemplating Jesus' teachings and striving to embrace His divine love and wisdom. May this book serve as a constant reminder that, no matter the circumstances, Jesus is with us, guiding us, and leading us every step of the way. May it be a blessing to you, and may it deepen your relationship with the One who is the Way, the Truth, and the Life.

Dr. Andrew C S Koh

Chapter 1
God of all comfort

Prayer

Heavenly Father, we pray for open, soft, receptive, teachable, and obedient hearts, in Jesus' name, Amen.

Setting

Paul revealed himself as the author of 2 Corinthians. He spelled out his credentials, an apostle of Jesus Christ by the will of God. Greek for apostle is *"apostolos,"* which means a messenger, someone sent out on a mission. Paul acknowledged Timothy, his co-worker, protégé, and spiritual godson in the faith. He identified his recipients as Christians in Corinth and Achaia. Corinth is the city. Achaia is the region or state. Christians are called saints. Greek for saint is *"hagio,"* which means holy, sanctified, or set apart. Paul's opening salutation was grace and peace. Grace is the common Greek greeting, *"charis"*. Peace is the common Hebrew greeting, *Justification precedes sanctification.* Grace precedes peace and grace precedes truth. Grace is the result of justification and peace is the result of reconciliation.

2 Corinthians 1: 3-7

3 Blessed be the God and Father of our Lord Jesus Christ, the Father of mercies and God of all comfort; 4 who comforts us in all our affliction, that we may be able to comfort those who are in any affliction, through the comfort with which we ourselves are comforted by God. 5 For as the sufferings of Christ abound to us, even so our comfort also abounds through Christ. 6 But if we are afflicted, it is for your comfort and salvation. If we are comforted, it is for your comfort, which produces in you the patient enduring of the same sufferings which we also suffer. 7 Our hope for you is steadfast, knowing that, since you are partakers of the sufferings, so you are also of the comfort.

Reflection

Greek for blessed is *"eulogeo"* which means praise. The English word eulogy is derived from the Greek word *"eulogeo"*. God, the Father of our Lord Jesus Christ, is the God of praise, mercies, and comfort. God comforts us in our suffering so that we can identify with and comfort other people who are suffering.

Christ comforts and restores us in our sufferings. Paul could identify with his audience because of his suffering. There is a higher purpose in suffering. Suffering helps us to help others in their suffering. Paul encouraged his audience to share in his suffering and consolation.

Application

There is a higher purpose in suffering. When we go through suffering, Christ comforts, rescues, and restores us. Suffering enables us to help others in their suffering. Suffering allows us to identify with other people's suffering.

Prayer

Heavenly Father, thank You for all that You have done for us in our lives. Thank You for delivering us from perilous, critical, and dangerous life situations. Thank You for rescuing us through the various storms of life. Thank You for delivering us in the past, in the present, and in the future, in Jesus' name, Amen.

Chapter 2
The just shall live by his faith

Prayer

Heavenly Father, may the words of our mouths and the meditations of our hearts be acceptable to You, in Jesus' name, Amen.

Setting

The law justifies no one. To be under the law is to be under the curse of the law. Law is legalism, and faith is grace. Those who obeyed the law will live by the law, but those who break the law will die by the law. The law cannot save sinners. Paul quoted Habakkuk 2: 4. The just shall live by his faith, in the finished work of Christ on the cross.

Romans 3:23, *"for all have sinned and fallen short of the glory of God"*.

Habakkuk 2:4, *"Behold the proud, His soul is not upright in him, but the just shall live by his faith"*.

Galatians 3:13-16.

13 Christ redeemed us from the curse of the law, having become a curse for us. For it is written, "Cursed is everyone who hangs on a tree, Deuteronomy 21:23, 14 that the blessing of Abraham might come on the Gentiles through Christ Jesus, that we might receive the promise of the Spirit through faith. 15 Brothers, speaking of human terms, though it is only a man's covenant, yet when it has been confirmed, no one makes it void or adds to it. 16 Now the promises were spoken to Abraham and to his offspring. He doesn't say, "To descendants", as of many, but as of one, "To your offspring, Genesis 12:7; 13:15; 24, which is Christ.

Reflection

Paul quoted Deuteronomy 21:23. Christ died on the cross as a substitutionary atonement for our sin. He redeemed us from the curse of the law. He was cursed so that we can be blessed. He paid the ransom for sin and saved us from the law. The promise of the Abrahamic covenant comes to the Gentiles through faith in Christ, Deuteronomy 21:23, his body shall not remain overnight on the tree, but you shall surely bury him that day, so that you do not defile the land which the Lord your God is giving you as an inheritance, for he who is hanged is accursed of God.

2 Corinthians 5:21, *For He made Him who knew no sin to be sin for us, that we might become the righteousness of God in Him.*

The Abrahamic covenant is an unconditional covenant between God and Abraham which no one can nullify. Abraham was a blessing to all the people on earth through his Seed, who is Christ.

The Mosaic law cannot nullify the Abrahamic covenant because the covenant preceded the Mosaic law by 430 years. The covenant was a promise, but the law was not.

Application

The law is not a channel for salvation. The law is a mirror that reflects sin. Without the law, you will not see your sin. Once you saw your sin and are convicted of sin, you come to Christ by faith. Christ paid the punishment for sin that you could not pay. All you need to do is believe in Him. It is by grace that you are saved through faith.

Prayer

Heavenly Father, we believe that You died on the cross to pay the punishment of our sin for us. We claim the promise that the just shall live by his faith in the finished work of the cross, in Jesus' name, Amen.

Chapter 3
Walking Bible

Prayer

Heavenly Father, we pray for understanding as we open Your inspired Word for us today in 2 Corinthians. We pray for illumination and anointing of the Holy Spirit. We permit You to search our hearts and motives. We pray that You will create in us a pure heart, in Jesus' name, Amen.

Setting

The Corinthians were Christ's letters written by the Holy Spirit on their hearts of flesh, not on tablets of stone.

The Mosaic law brings condemnation, but the Holy Spirit gives life.

The Mosaic law written on stone tablets resulted in death to those who broke it.

Moses' face shone with God's glory when he came down to meet the Israelites. He had to cover his face with a veil because the glory of God was too strong for the people even though it was fading away. In contrast, the Holy Spirit's glory is far greater than the glory on Moses' face.

2 Corinthians 3:12-18

12 Having therefore such a hope, we use great boldness of speech, 13 and not as Moses, who put a veil on his face, that the children of Israel wouldn't look steadfastly on the end of that which was passing away. 14 But their minds were hardened, for until this very day at the reading of the old covenant the same veil remains, because in Christ it passes away. 15 But to this day, when Moses is read, a veil lies on their heart. 16 But whenever someone turns to the Lord, the veil is taken away. 17 Now the Lord is the Spirit and where the Spirit of the Lord is, there is liberty. 18 But we all, with unveiled face seeing the glory of the Lord as in a mirror, are transformed into the same image from glory to glory, even as from the Lord, the Spirit.

Reflection

Moses covered his face with a veil because the Israelites could not tolerate to see the glory of God on his face. Until today, the veil still covered the hearts of Israelites and prevented them from understanding the revelation of Christ in the Old Testament.

One day, God will remove this veil and free the Israelites from spiritual blindness and make them believe in Christ. Christians who see the glory of Christ without any barriers will have their hearts transformed, and their minds renewed to become more like God.

Romans 12:2, *"And do not be conformed to the pattern of this world, but be transformed by the renewal of minds, that you may prove what is the good and acceptable and perfect will of God."*

Application

You are letters of Christ, not written in ink and paper, but by the Holy Spirit in your hearts. You carry the image and glory of Christ wherever you go. Non-Christians read your lives every day as though you are the "walking Bible". When people see you, will they see the glory of Christ? Are you the walking Bible that non-Christians read? You may be the only Bible that people will read.

Prayer

Heavenly Father, thank You for writing Your epistles into our hearts. Help us live our lives worthy of Your calling so that others may see the glory and image of Christ in us. Do not allow the world to squeeze us into its mold. Transform our hearts, renew our minds, and conform us into the image of Christ, in Jesus' name, Amen.

Chapter 4
The man with a withered hand

Prayer

Heavenly Father, we pray that You will help us unravel the text before us. We pray that You will help grow in spiritual maturity, attitude, character, personality, grace and knowledge in our Lord and Savior. Equip us to serve You in Your kingdom, in Jesus' name, Amen.

Setting

Jesus and his disciples were passing through a grain field on s Sabbath. The Pharisees charged the disciples for breaking the law when they plucked grains to eat. Jesus replied that even and his supporters ate the shew bread, which was reserved for the priest, 1 Samuel 1:21. Jesus proclaimed that He was the Lord of the Sabbath.

Luke 6:6-11

6 Now it happened on another Sabbath, also, that He entered the synagogue and taught. And a man was there whose right hand was withered. 7 So the scribes and Pharisees watched Him closely, whether He would heal on the Sabbath, that they might find an accusation against Him. 8 But He knew their thoughts, and said to the man who had the withered hand, "Arise and stand here." And he arose and stood. 9 Then Jesus said to them, "I will ask you one thing: Is it lawful on the Sabbath to do good or to do evil, to save life or to destroy?" 10 And when He had looked around at them all, He said to the man, "Stretch out your hand." And he did so, and his hand was restored as whole as the other. 11 But they were filled with rage and discussed with one another what they might do to Jesus".

Reflection

The Pharisees might have intentionally planted the man with a withered hand in the synagogue on that Sabbath to see if Jesus would heal him. If Jesus healed him, they could charge him for breaking the Sabbath.

Only Luke mentioned that it was the man's right hand that was withered. Luke was a doctor. His observation power was spot on. The Jewish leaders scrutinized Jesus. With omniscient knowledge, Jesus challenged them whether it was lawful to heal on a Sabbath. Since they remained silent, Jesus commanded the man to stretch out his right hand and when he did so, his hand was restored to normal. Instead of rejoicing at the miraculous healing, the Jewish leaders were incensed and plotted to harm Jesus.

Application

The Sabbatical laws cannot be applied to Jesus because He is Lord of the Sabbath. He instituted the Sabbath for the benefit of people so that they could rest one day per week.

The Jews convoluted the laws by adding the man-made traditions of the elders. Prohibitions for healing the sick were found in the traditions of the elders and not found in the Mosaic laws.

The man was under the oppression of satan for years due to this handicap. He could not experience Sabbatical rest with a withered hand. Now, for the first time in years, he rested! Restoration of health freed him from permanent disability and anxiety.

Jesus asked the man to stretch out his hand. This was something that he could not do because his hand was withered, deformed, and dried up. Despite this, the man stretched out his hand and was restored. The recipe for this miracle was faith and obedience. If Jesus asks you to do something which is impossible to do, will you obey and do it? Do you have faith in Jesus? With Jesus, nothing is impossible. All you need to do is to trust and obey because there is no other way.

Prayer

Dear God, we acknowledge that Jesus of Nazareth is the Lord of the Sabbath. Thank You for creating the Sabbath for our benefit so that we can have a day of rest every week to rest from our labour, to reflect on You, and to worship You. Thank You for freeing us from the slavery of sin, in Jesus' name, Amen.

Chapter 5
Beatitudes

Setting

Before choosing the 12, Jesus went to the mountain and prayed the whole night. After wrestling in prayer, He chose the 12 disciples. He prayed, selected the 12, and preached the sermon on the plains. Luke's sermon on the Plain was quite similar to Mathew's sermon on the Mount, although not identical.

Luke 6:20-23

20 Then He lifted up His eyes toward His disciples, and said: "Blessed are you poor, For yours is the kingdom of God. 21 Blessed are you who hunger now, for you shall be filled. Blessed are you who weep now, for you shall laugh. 22 Blessed are you when men hate you, and when they exclude you, and revile you, and cast out your name as evil, for the Son of Man's sake. 23 Rejoice in that day and leap for joy! For indeed your reward is great in heaven, for in like manner their fathers did to the prophets.

Reflection

These are the four beatitudes. Blessed are the poor, the hungry, the downtrodden, and the hated. The Greek word for bless in Greek is *"makarois"* which means to experience the fullness of God. The Latin word for bless is *"benedicat"* from which we get the word benediction. The reason for being poor, hungry, downtrodden and hated is because of persecution. Christians will be persecuted for the Son of Man's sake. Rejoice when persecuted because there is a promise of reward in the life to come.

Application

Blessed are those who realized how spiritually poor and bankrupt they are before a Holy God. Blessed are those who are mourning and crying because God will comfort them. Blessed are those who are hungry and thirsty for righteousness. Blessed are those who are hated and persecuted for Christ's sake because they will receive eternal life.

Prayer

Heavenly Father, thank You for instructing us in righteousness. Help us submit to Your Lordship and build our lives with You as our foundation. Help us bear good fruits, the fruit of the spirit. Help us to love the unlovable, the unloved, the downtrodden and the marginalized. Help us to love our enemies, bless those who curse us and pray for those who spite us, in Jesus' name, Amen.

Chapter 6
Born again

Prayer

Heavenly Father, we pray for Your presence in our journey into the general epistle of 1 Peter. We pray for the presence and anointing of the Holy Spirit to help us rightly divide the truth of Your Word, in Jesus' name, Amen.

Setting

Greek for begotten is "annagennao", which means born again. Christians are born again into a living hope to receive an eternal inheritance through Christ's resurrection from the dead, John 3:3 and 3:5. Our Heavenly inheritance is incorruptible, undefiled, divinely reserved, and preserved for us until Christ's second coming.

John 3:3, *Jesus answered and said to him, "Most assuredly, I say to you, unless one is born again, he cannot see the kingdom of God."*

John 3:5, *Jesus answered, "Most assuredly, I say to you, unless one is born of water and the Spirit, he cannot enter the kingdom of God.*

Peter encouraged his audience to be mentally prepared, clear-minded, and rest in the living hope of Christ's second coming. They should behave like obedient children free from greed and ignorance. They should be holy because God is holy, quoting Leviticus 19:2.

1 Peter 1:22-25

22 Since you have purified your souls in obeying the truth through the Spirit in sincere love of the brethren, love one another fervently with a pure heart, 23 having been born again, not of corruptible seed but incorruptible, through the word of God which lives and abides forever, 24 because "All flesh is as grass and all the glory of man as the flower of the grass. The grass withers and its flower falls away, 25 But the word of the Lord endures forever." Now, this is the word which by the gospel was preached to you.

Reflection

Peter reminded his audience that they were sanctified by the Holy Spirit to obey the truth. They should love one another with a sincere motive. They were born again by the power of the Holy Spirit through the incorruptible seed of the eternal Word of God. Peter quoted Isaiah 40:7-8. People are nothing more than perishable grass and flowers which are here today and gone tomorrow. In contrast, the Word of God is eternal and remains forever.

Isaiah 40:7-8, *"The grass withers, the flower fades because the breath of the Lord blows upon it. Surely the people are grass. The grass withers, the flower fades, but the word of our God stands forever."*

Application

You are born again by the Holy Spirit through the incorruptible seed of God's Word. You are born again to a living hope, to receive eternal inheritance of Christ through His resurrection from the dead.

You must rejoice even in times of sufferings, tribulations, afflictions, and trials because these tests of faith are more precious than gold.

Suffering produces perseverance, perseverance produces character, and character produces hope. You must be mentally prepared, clear-minded, and rest in the living hope of Christ. Your lives must be holy because God is holy. You are redeemed by the precious blood of Christ.

Romans 5:3-5, *"And not only that, but we also glory in tribulations, knowing that tribulation produces perseverance; and perseverance, character; and character, hope. Now hope does not disappoint, because the love of God has been poured out in our hearts by the Holy Spirit who was given to us".*

Prayer

Heavenly Father, thank You that we are born again by the power of the Holy Spirit through the incorruptible seed of Your living Word. We recognize that we are temporary and frail like grass and flowers, but Your Word is everlasting and will endure forever, in Jesus' name, Amen.

Chapter 7
Christ, the chief cornerstone

Prayer

Heavenly Father, we pray that You will speak to each one of us individually according to our unique situations and circumstances. Thank You for the ministry of Your word. We permit You to teach, convict, correct, train, and transform us into Your image, in Jesus' name, Amen.

Setting

We should set aside all malice, deceit, hypocrisy, envy, and evil speech. Having tasted the grace of God, we should crave, desire, and feed on the pure milk of God's word for spiritual maturity, growth, and nourishment. God's word is pure milk for our soul.

Jesus Christ is the chosen and precious chief cornerstone of God's spiritual temple that the Jewish leaders rejected. Christians are the living stones and holy priests of God's spiritual temple who offered their bodies as living sacrifices to God, Romans 12:1. Peter quoted Isaiah 28:16.

Romans 12:1, *"I beseech you therefore, brethren, by the mercies of God, that you present your bodies a living sacrifice, holy, acceptable to God, which is your reasonable service".*

Isaiah 28:16, *Therefore thus says the Lord God, "Behold, I am laying in Zion a stone, a tested stone, a costly cornerstone for the foundation, firmly placed. He who believes in it will not be disturbed".*

1 Peter 2: 7-10

7 Therefore, to you who believe, He is precious; but to those who are disobedient, "The stone which the builders rejected, has become the chief cornerstone," 8 and "A stone of stumbling, and a rock of offense." They stumble, being disobedient to the word, to which they also were appointed. 9 But you are a chosen generation, a royal priesthood, a holy nation, His own special people, that you may proclaim the praises of Him who called you out of darkness into His marvelous light; 10 who once were not a people but are now the people of God, who had not obtained mercy but now have obtained mercy.

Reflection

Christ is a precious stone to Christians but a stumbling and offensive stone to non-Christians. God's word is offensive to non-Christians who stumbled in disobedience. Peter quoted psalm 118:22.

Psalm 118:22, *"The stone which the builders rejected, had become the chief cornerstone".*

Christians are a chosen generation, a royal priesthood, a holy nation, God's own special people, who called them out of darkness into light. Peter quoted Hosea 2:23. In the past, we were not God's people, but now we were God's people. In the past, we did not receive God's mercy but now, we have received God's mercy.

Hosea 2:23, *Then I will sow her for Myself in the earth, And I will have mercy on her who had not obtained mercy. Then I will say to those who were not My people, "You are My people!" And they shall say, "You are my God!"*

Application

You must crave, desire, and feed on the pure milk of God's word to grow in the knowledge and grace of our Lord and Saviour. God's word is pure milk, living bread, living manna, and living water. Without God's word, your soul will be weak, stunted, unhealthy, and may even die.

You are the living stones and priests of God's spiritual temple. You are God's chosen generation, royal priesthood, holy and sanctified by the Holy Spirit. You must offer your body as a living sacrifice to serve God. You must offer your sacrifices of praise and spiritual gifts in kingdom service.

Prayer

Heavenly Father, thank You for the epistle of apostle 1 Peter that transcended time, culture, geography, and history. Even though Peter wrote this epistle 2000 years ago, it is still relevant and applicable to us in the 21st century. We pray for obedience, submission, and wisdom, in Jesus' name, Amen.

Chapter 8
A day is as a thousand years

Prayer

Heavenly Father, thank You for bringing us to the last chapter of 2 Peter. Even though this short epistle was written in antiquity, yet its message is profound, powerful, impactful, and applicable to every generation. We pray for wisdom in understanding, obeying, and applying, in Jesus' name, Amen.

Setting

We should have a high view of the Old Testament, written by the prophets, and the New Testament written by the apostles, including Peter. In the last days, skeptics and false teachers, who walked in the flesh, will deny and scoff at Christ's second coming.

These false teachers deny the creation narrative, Noah's flood, the final destruction of the world by fire, and the day of judgment for ungodly people.

2 Peter 3:8-9

8 But, beloved, do not forget this one thing, that with the Lord one day is as a thousand years and a thousand years as one day. 9 The Lord is not slack concerning His promise, as some count slackness, but is long suffering toward us, not willing that any should perish but that all should come to repentance.

Reflection

The Lord's delay in His second coming is the result of His patience because He is not willing that anyone should perish. His delay is to give time and opportunity for people to repent. God exists outside the time and space domain. He is omnipotent, omnipresent, and omniscient. He can see everything from everywhere from the beginning to the end at any moment in time. One day to the Lord can be as long as one thousand years to us. One thousand years to the Lord can be as short as one day to us.

Application

We need to have a high view of scripture viz. the Old Testament and the New Testament as these are God's inspired words for us.

We need to be faithful to Christ, live in peace with others, be above reproach and blameless in conduct and be patient in outlook.

Since we do not know when Christ will return, we should be prepared by living holy lives.

We should continue to grow in the grace and knowledge of our Lord and Saviour Jesus Christ by diligent Bible study and devotion.

Prayer

Heavenly Father, we know that Christ's second coming will be sudden, unexpected, and mysterious. He will destroy the world and recreate a new Heaven and a new earth. We ask You to help us grow in Your grace and knowledge, live holy lives and be ready for Jesus' return. In Jesus' name, Amen.

Chapter 9
Trials, temptation, and faith

Prayer

Heavenly Father, we come before You in submission and obedience, to listen to Your Word. We permit You to convict, correct, teach, train, and transform us into Your image, in Jesus' name, Amen.

Setting

In his opening salutation, James identified himself as the author. He spelled out his credentials, as a bond servant of God and the Lord Jesus Christ. He identified his recipients as those belonging to the twelve tribes of Israel scattered abroad. These were the messianic Christian Jews of the diaspora. Messianic Jews are Christian Jews who believed Jesus as their Messiah. These diaspora Jews were dispersed out of Jerusalem due to persecution by the hostile unbelieving Jews after the martyrdom of Stephen, Acts 8:1.

Acts 8:1, *"Now Saul was consenting to his death. At that time, a great persecution arose against the church which was at Jerusalem; and they were all scattered throughout the regions of Judea and Samaria, except the apostles."*

James 1:2-8

2 My brethren, count it all joy when you fall into various trials, 3 knowing that the testing of your faith produces patience. 4 But let patience have its perfect work, that you may be perfect and complete, lacking nothing. 5 If any of you lacks wisdom, let him ask of God, who gives to all liberally and without reproach, and it will be given to him. 6 But let him ask in faith, with no doubting, for he who doubts is like a wave of the sea driven and tossed by the wind. 7 For let not that man suppose that he will receive anything from the Lord; 8 he is a double-minded man, unstable in all his ways.

Reflection

James encouraged his audience, and us, to rejoice in the face of trials because trials are tests of faith. Faith produces patience, patience produces good works, and good works produce wisdom. He encouraged his audience, and us, to pray for wisdom with faith. To pray without faith is to be unstable and double-minded. The Greek word for double-minded is *"dipsychos"*, which means wavering between two opinions. Prayer without faith is superficial. Without faith, it is impossible to please God.

Application

We should rejoice when we face trials because trials are God's tests of faith. We should always be humble because life is so transient, fragile, unpredictable, and uncertain. God will reward us if we endure and overcome trials as Christians. We should be quick to listen, slow to speak, slow to anger, avoid immorality, wickedness, and believe in God's words with meekness.

Prayer

Heavenly Father, help us to lay aside all filthiness and wickedness and receive Your living Word with meekness. Help us control our tongue and speak words of blessing, kindness, encouragement, and life to others. Help us be doers of Your word, and not hearers of Your Word, in Jesus' name, Amen.

Chapter 10
The sin of discrimination

Prayer

Heavenly Father, thank You for ministering to us by Your Word of eternal life. We pray for receptive hearts, seeing eyes, listening ears, clear minds, and obedient spirits to receive Your Word. May the thoughts and meditations of our hearts be acceptable to You, in Jesus' name, Amen.

James 2:1-7

1 My brethren, do not hold the faith of our Lord Jesus Christ, the Lord of glory, with partiality. 2 For if there should come into your assembly a man with gold rings, in fine apparel, and there should also come in a poor man in filthy clothes, 3 and you pay attention to the one wearing the fine clothes and say to him, "You sit here in a good place," and say to the poor man, "You stand there," or, "Sit here at my footstool," 4 have you not shown partiality among yourselves, and become judges with evil thoughts? 5 Listen, my beloved brethren, has God not chosen the poor of this world to be rich in faith and heirs of the kingdom which He promised to those who love Him? 6 But you have dishonored the poor man. Do not the rich oppress you and drag you into the courts? 7 Do they not blaspheme that noble name by which you are called?

Reflection

We must not practice favoritism and discrimination. We must not give special attention to a rich man who wears fine clothing and expensive jewelry while despising a poor man who dressed shabbily to church.

Poor people are generally stronger in faith, and they generally trust and love God more than rich people. Rich people tend to trust in their wealth rather than in God. Generally, it is the rich people who oppress and drag the poor people to the courts, blaspheming the God who called them.

Application

There is no place for favoritism, discrimination, and racism in the kingdom of God.

We should love our neighbor as ourselves according to the 10 commandments, Leviticus 19:17. Showing favoritism is a sin because favoritism violates the commandment to love our neighbor. The law must be obeyed in its entirety. To break one law of the commandments is to break every law of the commandments.

Leviticus 19:18, *You shall not take vengeance, nor bear any grudge against the children of your people, but you shall love your neighbor as yourself, I am the Lord.*

Prayer

Dear God, help us not to discriminate against one another. Help us to consider all people as equal for in Christ, there is no rich or poor, male or female, Jews or Gentile, slaves or free. Everyone is equal and precious in Your sight. Help us to love our neighbors as ourselves, in Jesus' name, Amen.

Chapter 11
The sin of faith without work

James 2:14-20

14 What does it profit, my brethren, if someone says he has faith but does not have works? Can faith save him? 15 If a brother or sister is naked and destitute of daily food, 16 and one of you says to them, "Depart in peace, be warmed and filled," but you do not give them the things which are needed for the body, what does it profit? 17 Thus also faith by itself, if it does not have works, is dead. 18 But someone will say, "You have faith, and I have works." Show me your faith without your works, and I will show you my faith by my works. 19 You believe that there is one God. You do well. Even the demons believe, and tremble! 20 But do you want to know, O foolish man, that faith without works is dead?

Reflection

Justification is by grace through faith in Christ but doing good work is the response of God's love to save us. If someone has faith but refuses to do good works to assist the needy and the marginalized, their faith is dead.

Good work is the demonstration of genuine faith. Faith without work is not genuine faith. Christians are not the only people who believe in God. Even the demons believe in God and trembled on hearing His name.

Abraham's faith was accompanied by work. Abraham's justification was through faith and his faith was genuine because he was willing to sacrifice his son Isaac.

James did not advocate salvation by work righteousness. Good work is our response to justification by grace through faith in Christ. Genuine and living faith results in good work. James alluded to Joshua 2 regarding the faith of Rahab, the prostitute who protected the two spies.

Joshua 2:15-16, *Then she let them down by a rope through the window, for her house was on the city wall; she dwelt on the wall. And she said to them, "Get to the mountain, lest the pursuers meet you. Hide there three days, until the pursuers have returned. Afterward, you may go your way."*

Application

Justification is by grace through faith in Christ, but we respond to justification by doing good works out of gratitude to the saving grace of God. Faith without work is dead. Refusing to do good works to assist the needy and the marginalized is a sin.

Prayer

Heavenly Father, thank You for justification by faith. Help us to love our neighbor. Help us not to practice favoritism, discrimination, and racism. Help us demonstrate genuine faith by doing good works to help the poor and the marginalized, in Jesus' name, Amen.

Chapter 12
The sin of boasting

Prayer

Heavenly Father, we praise You and thank You. We give You all power, glory, praise, and honor. We acknowledged that Your name is above all names. We pray for wisdom, understanding, and insight to receive Your Word, in Jesus' name, Amen.

Setting

Wars, strive, conflicts, fights, and disagreements among people come from personal desires for power and covetousness.

We prayed but did not receive answers because we did not pray according to God's will. God is a jealous God who demands absolute loyalty. If we are friends with the world, we are enemies with God. Peter quoted Proverbs 3:34.

Proverbs 3:34, *Surely, He scorns the scornful but gives grace to the humble.*

We should submit by drawing near to God and resisting the devil. We should always be clear-minded and vigilant because the devil is ready to pounce on us like a roaring lion, 1 Peter 5:8. We are sinners with unclean hands and unclean hearts. We should purify their hands and hearts, mourn, weep, and humble ourselves before God.

1 Peter 5:8, *Be sober, be vigilant, because your adversary the devil walks about like a roaring lion, seeking whom he may devour.*

We should not criticize our Christian brothers or judge them by the law. We should obey the law and not judge others by the law.

James 4:13-17

13 Come now, you who say, "Today or tomorrow we will go to such and such a city, spend a year there, buy and sell, and make a profit"; 14 whereas you do not know what will happen tomorrow. For what is your life? It is even a vapor that appears for a little time and then vanishes away.

15 Instead you ought to say, "If the Lord wills, we shall live and do this or that." 16 But now you boast in your arrogance. All such boasting is evil. 17 Therefore, to him who knows to do good and does not do it, to him it is sin.

Reflection

We should not boast about tomorrow because we do not know what will happen to us tomorrow. Life is fragile, unpredictable, and transient, like the grass and flowers that are here today and gone tomorrow. Life is like a mist that appears for a short while and disappears. We should commit all our plans to God and acknowledge that only He knows what is best for us. Boasting is pride, arrogance, and evil. There is no place for boasting in the kingdom of God. Omitting to do good is a sin.

Application

We must pray according to God's will and draw closer to Him with submission and humility for Him to answer our prayers. God will answer our prayers if we have a living relationship with Him. We should never boast about tomorrow because life is uncertain, fragile, transient, and unpredictable. Instead, we should commit all plans to God and not boast about them.

20 years ago, I had a friend who had applied to migrate to New Zealand. The application was successful, and they had great plans. Unfortunately, his wife was suddenly found to have lung cancer and passed away within a few months. All their plans were shattered, but I am sure God knows what is best for them.

Prayer

Heavenly Father, help us submit to You and draw near to You in faith and humility. We pray to abide in You and Your word to abide in us. We acknowledged that we are sinners saved by grace. We pray for cleansing by the blood of Christ. Help us to humble ourselves in Your sight. We pray for uplifting our spirits and countenance, in Jesus' name, Amen.

Chapter 13
Decalogue

Setting

We have now reached the highest point in the book of Exodus. The LORD gave the ten commandments to the Israelites at Mount Sinai. The Hebrew word for ten commandments is Decalogue, which means ten words. The ten commandments consist of 2 tables. The first table consists of 4 vertical commandments directed to the LORD. The second table consists of 6 horizontal commandments directed to people.

The LORD gave the ten commandments by speaking directly to the Israelites without going through Moses as an intermediary. The LORD also wrote the ten commandments on two tablets of stone with His finger, and gave them to Moses, Exodus 31:18. The LORD reminded the Israelites again that He saved, rescued, redeemed, and delivered them out of Egypt. The first table of the ten commandments consists of 4 vertical commandments between God and the people. The LORD demands absolute devotion from the Israelites. They shall love the LORD with all their hearts, souls, and minds. They shall have no other gods, they shall not worship idols, they shall not misuse the name of God, and they shall obey the Sabbath because the LORD is a jealous God. God created the world in six days and rested on the seventh day. So, the seventh day or Saturday shall be a day of rest for the Israelites.

Exodus 31:18, When he finished speaking with him on Mount Sinai, he gave Moses the two tablets of the covenant, stone tablets, written with God's finger.

Exodus 20:12-17

12 "Honor your father and your mother, that your days may be long in the land which Yahweh your God gives you. 13 "You shall not murder. 14 "You shall not commit adultery. 15 "You shall not steal. 16 "You shall not give false testimony against your neighbor. 17 "You shall not covet your neighbor's house. You shall not covet your neighbor's wife, nor his male servant, nor his female servant, nor his ox, nor his donkey, nor anything that is your neighbor's."

Reflection

The second table consists of 6 horizontal commandments relating to relationships with other people. The first table dealt with loving God unreservedly. The second tablet dealt with loving others wholeheartedly. We must honor our parents, must not commit murder, must not commit adultery, must not steal, must not lie, and must not covet other people's possessions. Children who honor their parents will be blessed and will enjoy a long life.

Application

The LORD demands your total surrender and absolute devotion. Love God completely and follow Jesus every day by carrying your cross.

Matthew 22:37, *Jesus said to him, "'You shall love the Lord your God with all your heart, with all your soul, and with all your mind, Deuteronomy 6:5.*

Deuteronomy 6:6, *You shall love Yahweh your God with all your heart, with all your soul, and with all your might.*

Matthew 16:24-25, *Then Jesus said to his disciples, "If anyone desires to come after me, let him deny himself, take up his cross, and follow me. 25 For whoever desires to save his life will lose it, and whoever will lose his life for my sake will find it*

Prayer

Heavenly Father, thank You for giving us the ten commandments to the Israelites on Mount Sinai. Thank You for sending Your Son Jesus Christ to earth to live a sinless life and fulfill the law that we could never be able to do for ourselves. Thank You for justifying us by grace through faith in our Lord and Savior Jesus Christ. Help us to surrender our lives to You and make You the center of our lives, in Jesus' name, Amen.

Chapter 14
Wrestling with God

Setting

After executing the peace treaty ceremony with Laban, Jacob and his contingent left Paddan Aram and made their way back to Canaan. Twenty years ago, Jacob fled Canaan after deceitfully robbing Esau of Isaac's blessings. Twenty years ago, Esau threatened to harm Jacob as soon as their father Isaac died. Now, as Jacob was making his way back to Canaan, he was still terrified of Esau. This chapter ends with Jacob wrestling with God.

Jacob encountered an army of angels sent by God to protect him and his contingent, see Genesis 28:12.

Jacob called the place Mahanaim, which means two camps in Hebrews.

The messengers reported to Jacob that his brother Esau was coming to meet him with an army of four hundred men. Jacob was terrified when he heard about this. So, he divided his contingent into two companies, one in front and one at the back.

After this, he turned to the LORD in prayer. He called on the name of the Lord, claiming the promise of divine protection and blessing when he returned to Canaan. He acknowledged that he was not worthy of the LORD's blessing and grace. He prayed for the LORD to deliver him and his family from the hand of Esau. He claimed the promise of posterity.

To pacify Esau, Jacob instructed his servants to give Esau an enormous quantity of animals.

Jacob gave precise instructions to his servants to say to Esau that these were tokens of appreciation from his servant Jacob who was coming behind.

Genesis 32:24-28

Verses 24-28, 24 Jacob was left alone, and wrestled with a man there until the breaking of the day. 25 When he saw that he didn't prevail against him, the man touched the hollow of his thigh, and the hollow of Jacob's thigh was strained as he wrestled. 26 The man said, "Let me go, for the day breaks." Jacob said, "I won't let you go unless you bless me." 27 He said to him, "What is your name?" He said, "Jacob". 28 He said, "Your name will no longer be called Jacob, but Israel; for you have fought with God and with men and have prevailed."

Reflection

The LORD appeared to Jacob in the form of a theophany or Christophany and wrestled with him. Theophany is God appearing in a human form. Christophany is Christ appearing in a human form in His pre-incarnate state. Jacob wrestled with the LORD and refused to let Him go. The LORD touched and dislocated Jacob's hip, but Jacob refused to let go of his grip. Jacob was true to his name, which means heel snatcher in Hebrews. Jacob would not let go until the LORD blessed him. In response, the LORD changed Jacob's name to Israel. A change of name signified a change of character. Jacob means heel snatcher. Until now, the hallmark of Jacob's character was deception, greed, conniving, striving, grabbing, scheming, wheeling, and dealing. Israel means ruled by God. From now on, Jacob's life would be ruled by God and not by himself.

Jacob asked the LORD what His name was, but He blessed Jacob instead. Jacob named the place Peniel, which means, the face of God in Hebrews. Jacob walked with a limp as a reminder that he must lean on God and not on himself. Because of this passage of scripture, Jews until today considered the meat around the hip joint as non-kosher.

Application

The LORD changed Jacob's name from heel snatcher to rule by God. Did God change your name when you believed in Jesus?

After wrestling with God, Jacob finally surrendered his life to God. Have you surrendered your life to God?

Prayer

Heavenly Father, thank You for sending angels to take care of us and protect us from imminent dangers. Help us to surrender our lives to You and to make You the center of our lives. Thank You for forgiving us of our sins and salvation by grace through faith in Christ, in Jesus' name, Amen.

Chapter 15
This world is not our home

Prayer

Heavenly Father, Immanuel, Lamb of God, Lion of Judah, we confess that we are sinners. We believe that You died on the cross to pay the penalty of our sins. We surrender our lives to You and make You the centre of our lives, in Jesus' name, Amen.

Setting

Paul considered himself a work in progress. He was continuously running the spiritual race to win the victor's crown. Paul confessed that he did not understand every spiritual truth. Paul used the race metaphor to illustrate the Christian journey. When you run a race, you don't look back but run forward to reach the finishing line to win the prize. In our Christian race of life, we don't look back but run forward to reach the finishing line Heavenward. Let us walk the Christian journey of life as though we are running a race. Running the Christian race requires training in righteousness, perseverance, and endurance in the face of tribulations.

Paul exhorted the Corinthians, and us, to imitate him just as he imitated Christ.

1 Corinthians 11:1, *Imitate me, just as I also imitate Christ.*

Philippians 3:20-21, *20 For our citizenship is in heaven, from which we also eagerly wait for the Savior, the Lord Jesus Christ, 21 who will transform our lowly body that it may be conformed to His glorious body, according to the working by which He is able even to subdue all things to Himself.*

Reflection

Our real home is Heaven. We are only passing through this world as a sojourner. We are waiting for Jesus to come again, give us new perfect bodies, and take us back to Heaven with Him.

1 Thessalonians 4: 16-17, *"For the Lord Himself will descend from heaven with a shout, with the voice of an archangel, and with the trumpet of God. And the dead in Christ will rise first. Then we who are alive and remain shall be caught up together with them in the clouds to meet the Lord in the air. And thus, we shall always be with the Lord".*

Application

We are all works-in-progress. We are being sanctified and will continue to be sanctified until Christ's second coming. Sanctification is a life-long process by the Holy Spirit to make us more and more Christlike. Paul is our role model. We need to imitate Paul just as Paul needed to imitate Christ.

Prayer

Heavenly Father, help us to run the spiritual race of faith with perseverance and determination. Help us to be as tough and as disciplined as a soldier to fight the spiritual battle of faith. Help us to be as hardworking as a farmer to share the Gospel of peace, in Jesus' name, Amen.

Chapter 16
Healing a man with dropsy

Prayer

God, please help us overcome the fear of socializing and communicating with others because of the Coronavirus. Father, we need all the help from You as we are in uncharted territory. We commit today's devotion to You, in Jesus' name. Amen.

Luke 14:1-6

1 Now it happened, as He went into the house of one of the rulers of the Pharisees to eat bread on the Sabbath, that they watched Him closely. 2 And behold, there was a certain man before Him who had dropsy. 3 And Jesus, answering, spoke to the lawyers and Pharisees, saying, "Is it lawful to heal on the Sabbath?" 4 But they kept silent. And He took him and healed him, and let him go. 5 Then He answered them, saying, "Which of you, having a donkey or an ox that has fallen into a pit, will not immediately pull him out on the Sabbath day?" 6 And they could not answer Him regarding these things"

Reflection

The chief Pharisee invited Jesus for a Sabbath dinner. The dinner was set up by the Pharisees to trap Jesus. They deliberately planted a man with dropsy in the house on a Sabbath just like they planted the man with a withered hand in a synagogue, Luke 6:6-11.

One of the causes of dropsy or edema is due to heart failure. Other causes include nephrotic syndrome and liver cirrhosis. The Pharisees wanted Jesus to heal the man so that they could charge him for breaking the Sabbath. Their oral traditions forbade healing the sick on a Sabbath. Jesus challenged the validity of the oral traditions by asking, "is it lawful to heal on a Sabbath?". Since they kept quiet and refused to answer, Jesus proceeded to restore the man's hand by asking him to stretch out his hand. Ironically, the oral traditions allowed pulling a donkey out of a pit on a Sabbath but not healing a sick man.

Application

Jesus healing a man with dropsy on a Sabbath did not violate the Mosaic law. Healing the sick on a Sabbath is based on compassionate ground. The Mosaic law did not forbid this. It was their oral traditions that forbid this. Oral traditions are man-made laws.

Jesus superseded the Mosaic law because He is the Lord over the Sabbath. God gave the Mosaic law for the Israelite's benefit, but the Pharisees made the law very complicated and ridiculous but adding their oral traditions.

Prayer

Dear God, help us to trust You and obey You. Thank You that You are a miracle working God. Thank You that You are the God of the impossible. We pray that You increase our faith and help us with our unbelief, in Jesus' name, Amen.

Chapter 17
Who to invite for dinner

Setting

Seeing that guests were fighting for the best places to seat, Jesus told them a parable. He said, if anyone is invited to a wedding do not choose the best seat. Be humble enough to take the lowest seat. Whoever exalted himself will be brought low. Whoever humbled himself will be exalted. People need to be gracious, generous and humble. Great people are humble people.

Luke 14:12-14

12 Then He also said to him who invited Him, "When you give a dinner or a supper, do not ask your friends, your brothers, your relatives, nor rich neighbors, lest they also invite you back, and you be repaid. 13 But when you give a feast, invite the poor, the maimed, the lame, the blind. 14 And you will be blessed, because they cannot repay you; for you shall be repaid at the resurrection of the just.

Reflection

Jesus rebuked His host for inviting all the wealthy people for the dinner. Jesus said, when you invite anyone to a feast, do not invite the rich who can invite you back. Invite the social outcasts, the poor, the maimed, the lame, the blind, the marginalized who cannot invite you back. You will be blessed, and God will repay you at the end of time.

Application

When you invite friends for dinner, do not invite those who are in a position to invite you back. You should instead, invite the poor, and the marginalized who will not be able to reciprocate your kindness. The Lord who sees everything from heaven will reward you for what you do.

When someone invites you to a dinner, you should not look for the best seats. Choose whatever seat is available. Be gracious, generous, and humble.

Prayer

Dear God, help us to be gracious, generous, and humble. Help us to be kind to the poor, the weak, and the marginalized. Give us humble hearts and kind spirits. Help us not to be boastful in public places, in Jesus' name, Amen.

Chapter 18
The parable of the great feast

Setting

Jesus told them the parable of the great feast. The great feast is called the marriage supper of the Lamb. Those who are invited refused to come by giving lame excuses. The first said that he bought a land. The second said he bought an oxen. The third said he married a wife. Even today, people are still giving excuses for not coming to God.

Luke 14:21-24

21So that servant came and reported these things to his master. Then the master of the house, being angry, said to his servant, 'Go out quickly into the streets and lanes of the city, and bring in here the poor and the maimed and the lame and the blind.'22And the servant said, 'Master, it is done as you commanded, and still there is room.' 23 Then the master said to the servant, 'Go out into the highways and hedges, and compel them to come in, that my house may be filled. 24 For I say to you that none of those men who were invited shall taste my supper.' "

Reflection

The servant reported to the master that those invited to the feast rejected the invitation. Therefore, the master said, invite the street people, the poor, the maimed, the lame, and the blind. These people accepted the invitation with great joy. The master said, go to the highways and hedges, and invite even more people. The master represents God. This parable is directed to the Pharisees sitting at the table. Since the Pharisees rejected Jesus as their Messiah, the gospel went to the Gentiles who received it with great joy.

Application

The master represents God. The feast represents the Gospel. The first group of invitees represents the Pharisees or Jews. The subsequent groups of invitees represent the Gentiles. God gave the Gospel to the Jews but they rejected it outright. Because of this, God gave the Gospel to the Gentiles who accepted it with great joy.

Prayer

Dear God, thank You for inviting us to accept the good news of The Gospel. Thank you for saving us and justifying us by grace through faith in the finished work of Christ on the cross. Thank You that Christ died for us to pay the penalty of our sins for us. Thank You for the promise of eternal life, in Jesus' name, Amen.

Chapter 19
Salt

Setting

After dinner Jesus left the Pharisee's house, and a great multitude followed Him. He turned to the disciples and warned them about the cost of discipleship.

"If anyone comes to me and does not hate father and mother, wife and children, brothers and sisters—yes, even their own life—such a person cannot be my disciple. And whoever does not carry their cross and follow me cannot be my disciple." Luke 14:26-27

Jesus did not say that to be a disciple means to hate all his family members. This is hyperbolic (exaggerated) language. A disciple must love Jesus more than everything, including his family members.

He must be willing to carry his cross by denying himself and submitting to the Father's will.

He must count the cost of discipleship, pay the price and forsake all that he has. After this discourse, Jesus taught the disciples the lesson on salt.

Luke 14:34-35

34 "Salt is good; but if the salt has lost its flavor, how shall it be seasoned? 35 It is neither fit for the land nor for the dunghill, but men throw it out. He who has ears to hear, let him hear!"

Reflection

Salt is used as a preservative for meat and as a flavoring for food. Christians are called to be salt and light of the world. If Christians lose their saltiness, they cannot influence the world and will not be useful in the Kingdom of God. Christians are called to surrender all to Jesus. To be anything less is to lose their "saltiness".

Apart from salt, Christians are also the light to world. We are to shine to light of Christ to the non-believing community around us.

Application

Are you a salt of the world? Have you lost your saltiness? Salt is only good for use if it is salty. Your life must have the saltiness of Christ to influence non-Christians around you so that they will be attracted to Christ. Do not be tasteless and lukewarm.

Are you a light of the world? Do you reflect the light of Christ to those around you? Let your friends see the light of Christ through your testimony, behavior, and life style. Shine the light of Christ to brighten up the darkness of your community. Do not hide the light of Christ. Do not be a secret believer.

Prayer

Heavenly Father, thank You for inviting us to the marriage supper of the Lamb. We acknowledge that we are sinners saved by grace. We are not worthy to call You Lord. Please forgive us of our sins. Help us to be salt and light of the world. Salt to positively influence, and light to shine the glory of Christ in the community around us. Help us to be gracious, generous, and humble, in Jesus' name, Amen.

Chapter 20

I did it my way

Setting

Eleven years had passed between Genesis chapters 12 and 16. After eleven years, Abram and Sarai were still barren. They were impatient and could not wait for God to carry out His plan. They wanted to help God! Instead of trusting in God and waiting on Him, they went to work in the flesh. Abram and Sarah did it "my way" and things turned out really nasty, complicated, and messy.

Sarai told Abram to take her maid Hagar as his concubine. Abram agreed to it and Hagar conceived. Sarai in Hebrews means princess. Hagar in Hebrews means to run away. Abram took Hagar as a maid from Egypt in Genesis 12. After Hagar had conceived, she became proud and despised her mistress, Sarai.

Sarai blamed Abram for getting Hagar pregnant even though it was she who initiated the plan. Abram allowed Sarai to do whatever she wished with Hagar. Sarai mistreated Hagar until she ran away from the house.

Genesis 16:11-16

11 Yahweh's angel said to her, "Behold, you are with child, and will bear a son. You shall call his name Ishmael because Yahweh has heard your affliction. 12 He will be like a wild donkey among men. His hand will be against every man, and every man's hand against him. He will live opposed to all of his brothers." 13 She called the name of Yahweh who spoke to her, "You are a God who sees," for she said, "Have I even stayed alive after seeing him? The angel of the LORD found Hagar near a well on the way to Shur. 14 Therefore the well was called Beer Lahai Roi. Behold, it is between Kadesh and Bered. 15 Hagar bore a son for Abram. Abram called the name of his son, whom Hagar bore, Ishmael. 16 Abram was eighty-six years old when Hagar bore Ishmael to Abram.

Reflection

Most Bible scholars believed that the angel of the Lord was a Christophany, the pre-incarnate Christ who took on a human form. The angel of the Lord asked Hagar where she was from and where she was going. She replied that she was running away from her mistress Sarai. The angel of the LORD told Hagar to return to Sarai and submit to her. The angel of the Lord promised to multiply her descendants exceedingly.

The angel of the LORD told Hagar that she was pregnant and to name her son Ishmael. Ishmael in Hebrews means God listens. The angel of the LORD prophesied that Ishmael would be wild and aggressive to all his brothers. Hagar called the LORD, El Roi, which means, the God who sees in Hebrews.

Beer Lahai Roi, in Hebrews means the well of the living God. Hagar returned to Abram, delivered a son, and called him Ishmael. By now, Abram was eighty-six years old. Abram left Haran when he was seventy-five years old. Chronologically, 11 years had passed between Genesis 12 and Genesis 16.

Application

Abram and Sarai were impatient and did not wait upon the LORD. Abram and Sarai took matters into their own hands and did it their way. They used the Egyptian maid Hagar as a surrogate mother to conceive and deliver a child for them. This plan backed fire on them because it was not according to God's will. This caused so much hardship even until today, 4000 years later! If you do anything by the flesh and did not seek God's will, it will backfire on you. When God makes a promise, He will fulfil it in His own time and according to His own way. God has a divine clock. He is never too early, never too late but always on time. You need to wait on God to fulfill His plans for you.

Prayer

Heavenly Father, help us to have faith in You. Help us to understand that whatever You promise will come to pass at Your own time and in Your own ways. Thank You that You are never early, never late, but always on time. You are omnipotent, omnipresent, and omniscient. You know everything from the beginning to the end. You are the author and finisher of our faith, in Jesus' name, Amen.

One last thing

Thank you for selecting my book. I genuinely hope it has offered you an enjoyable and stimulating experience. I would appreciate your feedback and would be grateful if you could write a review on the platform where you bought it or on a book review site. Your feedback will help others make choices and show me which parts of the book were effective or lacking. Your honest review will help me grow as a writer and motivate me to create more engaging stories in the future.

Thank you once again for taking the time to explore my book. I genuinely hope it proved to be a rewarding experience for you. Your support means everything to me, and I am truly grateful to each reader who joins me on this journey. Together, we can cultivate a vibrant community of readers and writers united by our love for storytelling.

Each review contributes to a vibrant dialogue that enriches our literary experience. I look forward to hearing your thoughts and insights as we continue to explore the depths of creativity together. Your feedback is invaluable, and it inspires me to keep pushing the boundaries of my writing. Let's keep the conversation going and delve deeper into the stories that connect us all.

Dr Andrew C S Koh

Don't miss out!

Visit the website below and you can sign up to receive emails whenever Dr Andrew C S Koh publishes a new book. There's no charge and no obligation.

https://books2read.com/r/B-A-FMXV-YLILC

BOOKS 2 READ

Connecting independent readers to independent writers.

Did you love *The Way, the Truth, and the Life*? Then you should read *Bread of Life Daily Devotions*[1] by Dr Andrew C S Koh!

Dr. Andrew C. S. Koh brings readers Bread of Life, a powerful collection of 20 daily devotions based on 20 Bible passages. Each devotion begins with an opening pryaer, reflection, contemporary application, and a closing prayer. Drawing on his deep understanding and love of the scriptures, Dr. Koh encourages readers to read and meditate on the scriptures for themselves. With his deep insights, readers will gain a greater understanding of the context and background of each passage.

In Bread of Life, Dr. Koh presents a unique opportunity for the modern reader to gain greater wisdom and knowledge of the Bible. Dr. Koh's devotional offers readers a chance to pause and reflect on the timeless truths of the scripture and to apply them into their own life in

---

1. https://books2read.com/u/mZ0Bv5

2. https://books2read.com/u/mZ0Bv5

a meaningful and transformative way. With his thoughtful and engaging approach, Bread of Life is sure to become a favorite of readers who are seeking a daily devotional that is rooted in the scripture.

Bread of Life is a must-read for those seeking to deepen their understanding and appreciation of the Bible. Comparable to popular devotional books such as Max Lucado's "Grace for the Moment" and Richard J. Foster's "Celebration of Discipline," Dr. Koh's Bread of Life offers readers a unique and inspiring opportunity to explore the Bread of Life. Pick up a copy today and discover how Dr. Koh's daily devotions can uplift, encourage, and stimulate your faith.

Read more at https://www.drandrewcskoh.com.

Also by Dr Andrew C S Koh

Daily Devotion
Manna of Life: Daily Devotion

Daily Devotions
Bread of Life Daily Devotions
Words of Eternal Life
Bread From Heaven: Daily Devotions
Light of the World Daily Devotions
Light of the World Daily Devotions
The Way, the Truth, and the Life

Genesis
Understanding Genesis 1-11: From Adam to Abraham
Faith Journey of Abraham: Genesis 12-25
Life Story of Jacob: Genesis 26-36
The Story of Joseph: Genesis 37-50

Gospels and Act

The Gospel According to Matthew
Daily Devotion Gospel of Mark
The Gospel According to Luke
Daily Devotion Gospel of John
Acts: Volume 1 and 2, From Jerusalem to Rome
From Galilee to Golgotha

Non Pauline and General Epistles
Hebrews: the Just Shall Live by Faith
1 John, 2 John, 3 John & Jude: a Verse by Verse Bible Study
General Epistles: 1 Peter, 2 Peter, James

Pauline Epistles
Romans: The Just Shall Live by Faith
1 Corinthians
2 Corinthians
1 Thessalonians, 2 Thessalonians, Philemon
Pastoral Epistles: 1 Timothy, 2 Timothy, Titus
Galatians: Justified by Faith in Jesus Christ
Philemon: Charge to the Master's Account

Prison Epistles
The Prison Epistles
Philippians: Rejoice Always in the Lord
Colossians: He is the Image of the Invisible God
Ephesians: Every Spiritual Blessing in the Heavenly Places in Christ

Standalone

Apocalypse: Understanding the Book of Revelation
Expository Preaching
Memoirs of a Doctor
Moses: Let My People Go
The ABCS of Self-Publishing
Living Word Living Savior: a Portrait of Jesus Through the Eyes of John
From Stethoscope to Wisdom: Reflection of a Doctor
Walking in His Footsteps: A Pilgrim's Journey
Journey in Ryhme: Poems of Reflection
Mapping the Heart: The Doctor's Odyssey
The Forgotten Melody
Footprints in Time

Watch for more at https://www.drandrewcskoh.com.

About the Author

Dr. Andrew C. S. Koh is a Christian author who has published 36 books. Beyond his role as an author, he is also a blogger, podcaster, bible teacher, digital creator, and retired cardiologist. He pursued theology at Laidlaw College in Auckland, New Zealand in 1999. Currently residing in Malaysia with his family, he finds joy in coffee, travel, and photography. He is listed in the Malaysia Book of Records for having the Most Books Published and Released in 2021.

Find out more about Andrew on:

https://linktr.ee/andrewcskoh

Search Andrew's books on:

https://books2read.com/ap/xX066D/Dr-Andrew-C-S-Koh

Get your free books on:

https://storyoriginapp.com/giveaways/b295be58-7736-11ec-ac4b-e34d930c508e

https://books2read.com/u/3kYJlN

Read more at https://www.drandrewcskoh.com.

About the Publisher

Dr. Andrew C. S. Koh, a bestselling Amazon author, has authored 36 Christian books covering the New Testament, Old Testament, Bible study guides, and devotionals. Beyond his role as an author, he is a blogger, podcaster, bible teacher, and cardiologist. He pursued theology at Laidlaw College in Auckland, New Zealand in 1999.. Currently residing in Malaysia with his family, he finds joy in coffee, travel, and photography. He is listed in the Malaysia Book of Records for having the Most Books Published and Released in 2021.

Author of Memoirs of a Doctor:

https://dl.bookfunnel.com/hm2npovxom

Link Tree:

https://linktr.ee/andrewcskoh

Universal book link:

https://books2read.com/ap/xX066D/Dr-Andrew-C-S-Koh

New Release Notification:

https://books2read.com/author/dr-andrew-c-s-koh/subscribe/1/384961/

Free Books:

https://storyoriginapp.com/giveaways/b295be58-7736-11ec-ac4b-e34d930c508e

https://books2read.com/u/3kYJlN

Read more at https://www.drandrewcskoh.com.